Copyright © 201⏃ ⏃⏃ ⏃⏃⏃⏃⏃⏃ ⏃⏃⏃⏃⏃⏃⏃⏃

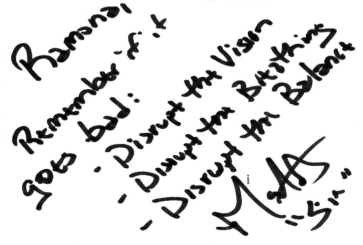

Disclaimer and Release from Liability

Self-Defense and Martial Arts training are dangerous and can cause serious injury or death. Particular care should be taken when executing techniques against vital strike areas such as eyes, nose, throat, groin, solar plexus and any areas that incapacitate or may cause death.

One should also be aware of the use of force laws when defending oneself or others. In many states it is unlawful to use more force than the force being used against you. It is advisable to consult an attorney to better understand the laws where you live, work or travel. Care should be taken during training or when performing the techniques, as well as during an actual self-defense encounter.

By receiving and/or reviewing this book, or by participating in subsequent classroom or live self-defense training, it is agreed that the writers, instructors, trainers, Panther Protection Services and Samurai Publishing are not liable for its contents and/or the subsequent use or misuse of the materials or techniques discussed.

The writers, instructors, trainers, company, range, dojo or other facilities are held harmless and released from liabilities, any cause of action, civil or criminal, which may result due to use, negligence, misconduct, or misuse of course materials and instructions.

Acknowledgements

Thank you to all of you who gave of your time in helping pull this project together. May God continue to bless and watch over you. Special thanks to the lovely and dangerous Lana Fallon; you could be a Bond girl! Much gratitude to Agent Butts, Sensei Kenneth Mitchell (1st Dan), Sensei Mitch O'Neal (2nd Dan) and Grand Master Leonard Holifield (10th Dan) for your assistance. Thank you Mike Smith and Renee James-Gilmore for your photographic contributions.

To my lovely and talented daughter Jasmyne, I am so proud of the lady you have become. No father could have a daughter more caring and loving than you! From the moment I heard your heartbeat in the womb I knew ensuring your well being would be the highest priority in my life.

Lana Fallon
Common Sense Self-Defense Student

Lana Fallon is a triple threat. She is an accomplished singer, writer and producer. She has toured the world, collaborated with a number of artists on multiple projects and is as comfortable behind the microphone as she is running the sound board.

Like many women I've trained, Lana came to a realization-personal protection is essential for pursuing a healthy, well balanced life in a world shared by unbalanced individuals. Lana had never had a physical altercation or previous self defense training when she began working with me on this project. That said, she was all too familiar with the unwelcomed advances women face sometimes by strangers, and sometimes by people who hold themselves out as friends. She was a perfect student for me to structure the concepts and techniques contained in this book because she understands what real life women face as they endeavor to be open and accepting, but capable of handling threats in the environment.

Because she has trained and continues to practice, Lana has become quite a force to be reckoned with on the stage and on the street.

You can learn about Lana by visiting www.lanafallon.com

TABLE OF CONTENTS

Understanding the Book

My objective is to increase your awareness of risks and threats. We want to give you effective countermeasures against threats. Most importantly I hope to enhance your ability to prevail in the event of an attempted assault.

At the start of each chapter on defensive techniques are everyday real life events that serve to caution. We or someone we love may stand just a moment away from a life altering situation. You probably are aware of ladies who have experienced similar circumstances.

The book is designed to give readers a greater understanding of self-defense concepts. It should be used as a study aid and reference. It is an introduction to self-defense techniques. Its limited scope in some cases prohibits more detailed explanations. Please make time to master the techniques outlined. Stay aware, stay focused and stay safe! God bless.

Risk reduction is like self esteem, it doesn't need anyone's permission but yours.

Chapter 1
Understanding the Threat

The U.S. Department of Justice estimates that 1 in 5 college women will be raped at some point during a five year college career.

Understanding the Threat

Common Sense Self-Defense - "A Woman's Self-Defense Survival Guide"

Self-defense is not a sport or an exercise video, it is a way to protect yourself and potentially survive an unwelcomed encounter. Women who are attacked are often not prepared to defend themselves. This instruction is designed to introduce and give you basic skills that may help you stay alive in the case of an attack. In the event of an attack the main objective is to stop the assault and get away. The techniques in this book when used properly can help you stop an assault.

Our defense concepts are simple and focus on the tried and true elements of traditional martial arts training. Attack the weaker parts of the aggressor's body with the stronger parts of yours. Learning to put something hard on something soft will serve you well (elbow to the nose, knee to the groin or kidneys, finger to the eye).

Our defense strategies are strength, size and gender neutral. The main focus of our training centers on attacking a perpetrator's vital areas such as eyes, nose, ears, throat, groin, and solar plexus. These are highly sensitive parts of the body that remain vulnerable no matter the perpetrator's strength or size.

Understanding the Threat

Common Sense Self-Defense focuses on:

- Basic and intermediate self-defense skills (strikes, escapes, improvised weapons and verbal commands)
- Characteristics of an attacker
- Characteristics of a victim
- Strategies to decrease your odds of being attacked
- Strategies to increase your odds of survival if you are attacked

Risk reduction is like self esteem, it doesn't need anyone's permission but yours. Take control. Empower yourself!

Understanding the Threat

Basic Principle

The most fundamental principle of women's self-defense is the identification of potentially dangerous situations **before** they occur. This awareness of environment is the best source of prevention. I believe most male attackers are cowards masquerading as bullies. They want to take valuables that they themselves are too weak or gutless to earn. Sometimes the valuable is a purse full of credit cards. Sometimes the valuable is someone else's self esteem or promising life. That brand of coward attacks a woman if he feels he has an advantage and he won't get caught.

Conscious awareness of potential threats in an environment is a source of control for a woman. Conversely, a woman is at risk of becoming victimized when she becomes comfortable walking alone in such places as a workplace parking lot without considering the possibility of an attack each and every time she enters that area.

Be aware. Be alert. Begin employing this basic principle by not leaving situations to chance. Do not take for granted the dangers that may await the unsuspecting who enters a parking lot or isolated stairwell alone. Seriously consider the possibility that a perpetrator could be hiding there.

Be alert to the reality that crime does not happen only after dark. Make it your habit to take basic preventive steps such as asking someone to walk with you in parking lots. Instead of politely declining a grocery store employee's offer to carry your bags to your car, say "yes" in instances when you are unprepared to protect yourself. Determining whether you

Understanding the Threat

are prepared or unprepared requires consciously assessing the environment and acting accordingly. Basic preventative measures such as crossing to the other side of a street when someone suspiciously approaches only cost a little of your time. Avoiding a dangerous situation is a primary tool in an effective personal defense arsenal.

Women can reduce the potential of being victimized by exercising risk reduction measures such as:

- Be alert in familiar locations, as well as in unfamiliar sites. Do not invite danger by hitchhiking or going to dangerous places unprotected. If you and a child are at a bus stop and someone unknown offers a ride, think twice. This is a spin on hitch hiking.
- Always make sure someone else knows where you are going on a date and with whom. Preferably, let another know what you are wearing so that you may be identified.
- Trust your senses. If something makes you feel uncomfortable, don't be afraid to leave a date and take a taxi or call a friend to pick you up. You don't need permission to control your sense of safety.
- Don't park next to vans or other high vehicles such as SUVs. It is easy to be pulled into one by a criminal.
- Be alert to the perils of drinking alcohol in excess. In addition to the risks associated with driving under the influence, alcohol impairs judgment and motor skills. The ability to protect oneself and to make sound decisions can be compromised by alcohol and drugs- including certain over-the-counter pharmaceuticals.

Understanding the Threat

When you plan to interact with other people take heed to labels on medications that warn of temporary impairment.

- Never leave your glassware unattended at a bar, restaurant or party. With of the proliferation of 'date rape' drugs, an unattended glass begs for a victim.
- Do not walk around with expensive jewelry or handbags in unfamiliar neighborhoods or countries.
- Always, always lock the doors of your car and keep your cell phone within reach when you are comfortably in your car. This applies whether you are in your home's driveway or stopped at a traffic light.
- Don't use busy places such as supermarket or mall parking lots as a vanity to put on your makeup or casually chat on your cell phone. These type areas are too vast to monitor while you're multi-tasking.
- Avoid using headphones in public places. If you decide to use headphones while you're on an airplane, jogging, or at your office desk make sure you can hear environmental sounds around you.
- Avoid isolated stairwells. They are choice locations for criminals.
- Be very sure of your parking location, particularly in parking decks. Wandering around marks you as an easy target.
- Don't pull up closely to a car in front of you when stopping at a red light or stop sign. Doing so impedes your ability to evade and make a quick escape. If you cannot see the rear tires in front of you, you probably don't have enough turn radius to escape.

Understanding the Threat

- Always have the appropriate key in your hand for quick access into your car, home or office.
- Use a valet key for its intended purpose and avoid giving a restaurant or hotel valet your full set of keys. Access to your full set of keys grants access to your car trunk, office and home.
- Know how to activate the GPS on your cell phone and be alert to the fact that when a GPS is active good guys and bad guys can identify your whereabouts. You need law enforcement to know your whereabouts in the event of a kidnapping. You do not want a stalker to track you. Use the instrument in a way that works for you based upon your circumstances.
- Have an *In Case of Emergency* (ICE) category on your cell phone.

Prepare to utilize improvised weapons to assist in a defense. Almost everything can be a weapon. A key, hair pin, salt shaker or fork can ward off an attacker. Stab at his eyes, ears, throat or groin until the perpetrator lets go. Mace and pepper spray are popular self-defense weapons. However, they must be in your hand and sprayed directly into the attacker's face to be most effective. Target practice and a conscious effort to keep mace or pepper spray in-hand are required for them to be effective tools. Take a moment today to look around your home, car, office and wardrobe to identify potential improvised weapons. We will cover the use of improvised weapons in greater detail later in Chapter 11.

Understanding the Threat

Understanding the Perpetrator – The Surprising Story Behind the Victim Numbers

Women are more likely to be murdered by someone familiar than by a stranger. Relationships that were deteriorating or that ended badly have resulted in the demise of women who mistakenly believed they could simply walk away. Crime data provides surprising evidence of the frequency with which women are harmed by men known to them. Though it seems counterintuitive, women are most often killed by people who professed love or attraction. Being attuned to the environment includes being alert to the peculiarities of

Understanding the Threat

familiar people who share our space. According to Bureau of Justice statistics[1]:

- Females are generally murdered by people they know. In 64% of female homicide cases, females were killed by a family member or intimate partner.
  *24% of female homicide victims were killed by a spouse or former spouse.
  *21% were killed by a boyfriend or girlfriend.
  *19% were killed by another family member.
  *25% of females were killed by others they knew.
- Females made up 70% of victims killed by an intimate partner.
- Females were killed by intimate partners at twice the rate of males.
- Black female victims of intimate partner homicide were twice as likely as white female homicide victims to be killed by a spouse.
- Black females were four times more likely than white females to be murdered by a boyfriend or girlfriend.

It is also worthy of noting that statistics indicate 48% of all crimes committed in the U.S. were violent crimes against people, while 38% were crimes against property[2]. Based on those statistics, crimes against

---

[1] Source: Bureau of Justice Statistics/Selected Findings- Female Victims of Violence, Revised October 23, 2009

[2] The Bureau of Justice statistics regarding violent crime included rape/sexual assault, robbery of people, aggravated and simple assault. Crimes against property included household burglary, theft and motor vehicle theft.

Understanding the Threat

individuals are reported with greater frequency than crimes against property. Each one of us has only one life to live. Our attention is on limiting the impact of assaults on people as we go about our lives. Inanimate objects can be replaced.

Rape is one of the most dehumanizing crimes of violence. The outrage of rape is often compounded by other violent, sexually assaultive types of crime, such as forced oral copulation, forced sodomy and rape by instrumentality.

Understanding the Threat

There is a misconception about sexual assault. It is mistakenly believed that all rapists are overcome with sexual desire. Even in the 21st century some think that a woman who is raped may have dressed too seductively or "asked for it" in some manner. These ideas assume that rape is purely a sexual act, a crime motivated by desire. Yet, in many cases rape is purely a violent crime, a hostile takeover, an attempt to hurt and humiliate. Sex is used as a weapon. A rapist will use that weapon against friends, strangers, and acquaintances of all ages, races and body types.

There is no single right way to stop an attack. Do what you can, but the most important thing is to survive.

While violence against women happens every day and all around us, a significant number of women continue to take a very passive approach to protecting themselves from a potentially violent encounter. They do not insure themselves against crimes upon their person by learning personal protection techniques. Would you advise someone you care about to neglect insuring her automobile or home because an accident may not happen? It is surprising that we take time to protect material assets against loss but most of us fail to insure the family's greatest asset- your safety!

Understanding the Threat

Relationship DANGER signs:

Professing love in the earliest stages of a new relationship and attempting to sweep you off your feet with an over abundance of considerate acts is the number one sign of a potentially battering relationship. The premature timing of this expression is a warning sign that you may be facing a manipulating personality in the admirer. Be alert to relationship danger signs:

- Extreme jealousy. Warning signs include your partner's desire to limit your interaction with other friends; thinking everyone around desires intimacy with you; expecting you to spend every second with

Understanding the Threat

him. Extreme jealousy isn't a compliment; it's a problem.

- Controlling Behavior. Warning signs include keeping track of whom you're with and where you are; telling you what to wear; choosing your friends; keeping you from getting a job or interfering with your work; taking your money; threatening to commit suicide; threatening to spread gossip or tell secrets about you. Violence among lesbian and gay couples is believed to be under-reported due to trepidation associated with publicly acknowledging a homosexual relationship.

- Violent Actions. Violence can be mental, sexual or physical in form. Warning signs include cruel insults; isolating you from family and friends; imposing unwelcomed sexual activity; hurdling intimidating remarks; intentionally embarrassing you in the presence of friends.

- Veiled Threats. Joking about posting images of you in nude or compromising positions may actually be a concealed threat. If it's talked about it has been thought about. Other warning signs include awkward or left-handed compliments; remarks about inviting authorities such as children's services or a probation officer to visit with you.

- Mis-directed Blame. Don't allow a partner to treat you as though his problem is your fault. Blaming you is a good indicator that attempts will be made to 'fix' you as it is natural to correct problems.

Understanding the Threat

Be realistic. While it is possible for a partner's bad behavior to change, don't stay in a bad situation expecting a metamorphosis. If you need assistance to get away call 911 or the National Domestic Violence Hotline:

1-800-799-7233 (SAFE)

Assaults, home invasions, car-jackings, abductions, rapes and other forcible felonies are life altering experiences. A plethora of data sources confirm repeating occurrences of these crimes at home and abroad. Crime is not isolated to strangers in towns unknown to us. Just plug into what's happening in your neighborhood for confirmation. News about a tough economy; studies concerning the desensitization of youth to violence; reports of terrorist acts within the American homeland; and evolving technologies used by professional predators beg the question: How prepared am I to defend myself or my family?

It is often said self-defense is a mindset. As an Executive Protection Specialist (bodyguard) and Combatives Instructor, I caution that the mindset without practical defensive skills is a hallucination. In the upcoming chapters we will introduce defensive techniques and principles to help increase your ability to survive an assault and get away.

Chapter 2
Preparing to Defend

Training introduces you to concepts, but only practice builds skills!

Preparing to Defend

Understanding the Tool of Violence

Violence is the tool of preference for aggressive criminals who steal valuables that they themselves are too weak or spineless to earn. This chapter explores the use of violence as a tool that law abiding citizens can exploit. Women who trained with me say their confidence increased once they actualized the following concept: Violence is a tool women can exploit for personal protection.

Violence itself is neutral, as violence is nothing more than *focused aggression*. All violent acts involve a person committing violence and a person receiving the violent act. A woman who is prepared to deliver a *violent reaction* to an aggressor improves her chances of survival.

The most important tool for self-defense is avoidance. Constantly assess your environment and try to stray from harm's way. However, in the face of imminent harm *your* use of *focused aggression*—violence—may save your life!

Cowards and criminals embrace violence as a tool to oppress, control, and rob. Law abiders should not be so naïve as to ignore violence as a tool in their self protection arsenal. Genuine empowerment occurs when a law abider masters her use of violence as a protection tool. If her response to aggressive stimuli is equally aggressive, she increases her chances of maintaining her true valuables-life, safety, self esteem. That is why so much attention in self-defense circles is on attacking the attacker.

Preparing to Defend

Let me be crystal clear on a point. Generally, the person committing violence prevails. Consequently, to survive an encounter a woman must be well prepared to act in a manner that is contrary to the nurturing impulse. A woman must use her own *focused aggression* in a manner that combines the natural instinct for self-preservation with ingrained techniques for neutralizing threats. Self-defense training aids in mastering the techniques. In a self-defense situation you must be prepared to cause *injury*, as well as receive injury.

We'll explore a few basic principles of self-defense. There is a difference between hitting which produces non specific trauma versus hitting that inflicts injury. The body can take a lot of abuse; however it doesn't do well under *focused aggression*. This principle explains why a professional boxer such as Lela Ali can still stand after many rounds of taking blows across the body, yet fall after 15 seconds of strategically placed hits. When injury is inflicted, it's over.

A woman who inflicts *injury* upon an attacker may give herself time to escape. Injury can force an aggressive attacker to stop and experience 'pain compliance,' giving the woman time to run.

Running away is also a basic principle. However, consider that inflicting injury upon an attacker may be necessary for an escape. Inflicting injury may be essential to keeping an attacker from running after you. Injury helps negate mass. This principle explains why a woman of average stature can immobilize a bigger, stronger man.

Preparing to Defend

At the point of violence there should be a singular focus, prevailing! Unless you are 100% sure you can get away from an attacker, serious consideration should be given to using the tool of violence as "Plan B".

Experienced personal protection professionals do not condone the use of violence as a first line of defense. Instead, we encourage law abiders to gain an understanding regarding how and when the tool of violence may be exploited for safety purposes. We learn from the animal kingdom that predators seek easy prey. Don't be easy.

Preparing to Defend

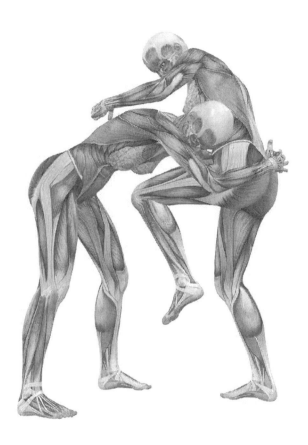

Preparing to Defend

Strikes

Striking means to select a focus point and throw your body weight behind it. The fist is a focus point that we are introduced to as early as childhood. Some of us were told, "If he hits you, hit him back as hard as you can." Instructions to this effect are flowing from the mouths of youth somewhere in America even at this moment.

As we move through adulthood oftentimes there has been little more instruction than what we heard as children. Fighting is a learned skill and not a core competency of the masses. Throughout my years working in the corporate world, I didn't meet many people who included "learn hand to hand skills" in their development plans. As we mature and gain awareness of how easily we or loved ones might fall prey to the criminal element, it makes common sense to enhance our self-defense skills. Understanding the full complement of focus points on the human body and how to strike properly adds to one's arsenal of self-defense tools.

A concept I teach during self-defense training sessions is "put something hard on something soft." More about strikes and the concept of "put something hard on something soft" is explained in this chapter.

Adults with limited defense training, whether male or female, should avoid striking using the conventional fist position. People with minimal combative experience and training often break their hands in physical confrontations because they have not learned how to make a proper fist.

Preparing to Defend

Additionally, some women are unable to make a proper fist due to the length of their finger nails.

To increase defense capabilities while minimizing potential injury to ourselves, using alternatives to striking with the conventional fist is highly encouraged. Effective alternatives are identified in the concept of "put something hard on something soft." Study the accompanying graphics which display many of the striking methods we endorse for self-defense.

Use parts of your anatomy that are hard for the purpose of hitting an adversary's soft tissue. Here's an example. If you deliberately focus on thrusting your elbow to strike a perpetrator's eye, which is largely soft tissue, you will undoubtedly change his channel immediately upon contact.

The "put something hard on something soft" concept also applies to using the harder parts of your anatomy to move a perpetrator's joint into an abnormal position. No matter the towering size of an adversary, if you disrupt his balance by breaking or dislocating his knee or ankle he won't be much of a threat at that point. One way of breaking a predator's knee is with a swift kick directly on the knee; you may also dislocate the patella or knee cap with a swift kick to the side of the knee. A thumb, two extended fingers or a chop to the trachea will adversely impact the attacker's breathing. This "put something hard on something soft" tactic maximizes your escape efforts because injuring soft tissue or manipulating a joint on an adversary's body does not require you to have exceptional strength.

Preparing to Defend

Described below are some focused striking points. Combine these hard parts of the human anatomy with the defense techniques reviewed in this book to enhance your ability to neutralize a threat and maximize your chances of not being victimized:

- Elbow Strike
- Head Butt
- Inside of the Forearm
- Knees
- Knife Hand
- Palm Heel
- Ridge Hand

The concepts are simple:

- Disrupt the Vision

- Disrupt the Breathing

- Disrupt the Balance

Any combination of the above is good for you and bad for him!

Preparing to Defend

Palm Heel Strike

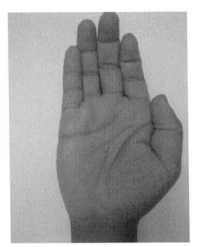
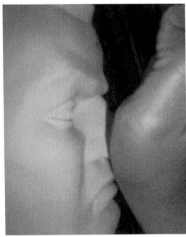

Ridge Hand Strike

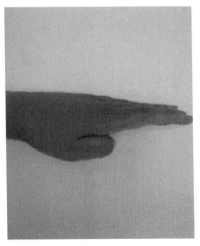

Preparing to Defend

Knife Hand Strike

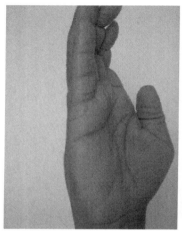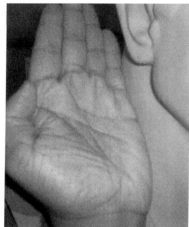

Elbow Strike

Preparing to Defend

Knees

Head Butt

Preparing to Defend

Nerve and Vital Points

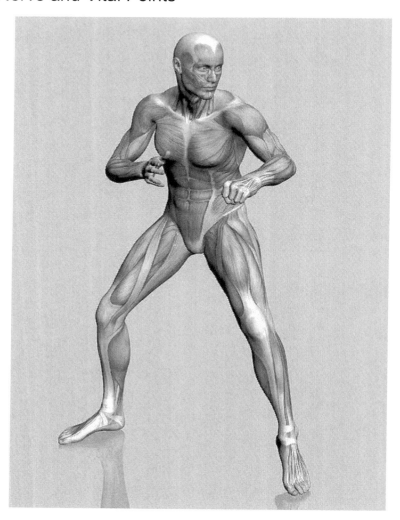

Preparing to Defend

Nerve and Vital Points

- Ankle
- Back of Ear and Base of Skull
- Back of Hand
- Back of Neck
- Biceps
- Calf
- Carotid Artery
- Chin
- Collar Bone
- Ear
- Eyes
- Forehead
- Forearm Muscle
- Groin
- Jaw
- Nose
- Outside of Thigh
- Side of Neck
- Suprascapular Nerves (front of shoulders)
- Temple
- Throat
- Top of Head
- Under the Nose

Preparing to Defend

Perpetrator Impact Zones

Earlier in this chapter the term "striking" was defined. Striking means to select a focus point and throw your body weight behind it. This chapter also introduces "impact zones." A woman in a struggle creates an advantage for herself when she targets a perpetrator's impact zones. Attacking "impacts zones" is a more efficient use of energy and is far more effective than hitting arbitrarily at an opponent.

An impact zone is an area of the anatomy that is highly susceptible to injury upon a strike. Areas of soft issue and joints are considered as impact zones because they are prone to injury when absorbing pressure from a strike. Strikes to a perpetrator's impact zones are highly effective in causing injury. A perpetrator's eye, throat, shin, finger or knee would be an impact zone to strike in a struggle. Strike as many impact zones as possible and as quickly as possible. Training and practice in striking impact zones will increase your capacity to defend yourself or a loved one.

In addition to those already mentioned, this chapter includes a list of impact zones. Study the terms, review the graphic demonstrations in subsequent pages and train with a self-defense professional to maximize your efficiency. Practice is a key element of defense training. It enhances your ability to prevail.

Preparing to Defend

Ankle/Instep – A strike to this area can result in broken bones.

Armpit - A strike to this area can result in muscular damage, cramping or numbness in the side. Accompanied by a protruding knuckle, a strike to the armpit is particularly painful.

Back (mid-lower back/third lumbar vertebra) – A strike to this area can result in broken bones, paralysis or death.

Buttocks (lower) - A strike to this area can result in muscular damage, cramping or numbness in the lower leg.

Carotid Artery – A moderate blow causes pain and stuns temporarily. A heavy strike to this area may result in unconsciousness.

Chin (under the) – A moderate strike can cause the head to snap back and put an attacker off balance. A heavy strike can cause unconsciousness.

Clavicle – A strike to this area can result in broken bones and disabling of the arm.

Coccyx – A strike to the coccyx, commonly known as the tail bone, can result in broken bones and numbness to the legs.

Ear –A moderate strike can cause pain and disorientation. A heavy strike may injure the inner ear and cause loss of balance.

Preparing to Defend

Ear (under the) – The hollow behind the ear is a pressure point. Pain and injury can result by grinding a thumb or knuckle into the area.

Elbow Joint (inside of) – A strike to this area will bend the arm and cause pain. A forceful strike will bend the arm and cause pain similar to the sensation felt when hitting your funny bone.

Elbow (outside of) –Strikes to this area can cause hyperextension and an injury or tear to cartilage. A cartilage tear incapacitates the arm and requires surgery to repair. A heavy strike can cause a break.

Eyes – Even a slight strike to the eyes can cause serious or permanent injury. Strikes to the eyes result in impairment and may cause blindness.

Fingers - A moderate strike or bend to a finger can cause bruising and pain. A heavy strike can result in a fracture or inability to use the hand.

Floating Rib – A strike to this area can disrupt breathing and result in broken bones, internal injuries or death. A fractured rib can rupture a kidney.

Forearm Mound (inside) – A strike to this area causes considerable pain and numbness.

Forearm Mound (outside) – A strike to this area causes considerable pain and numbness to the forearm flexors.

Preparing to Defend

Groin – A strike to an unprotected groin area will result in debilitating pain. Strikes to this area may also render reproductive organ damage or unconsciousness.

Kidney – A strike to this area can result in internal injuries or death.

Knee – A strike to this area can result in dislocated or broken bones.

Knee (back of) – A strike to this area can bend the knee or result in dislocated bones.

Larynx – A strike to this area can result in extreme pain and grasping for air. Temporary or permanent damage to the voice box may result from a strike to the larynx. A heavy strike can result in death.

Neck (cervical vertebra) – A strike to this area can result in broken bones, paralysis or death.

Nose (bridge of) – A moderate strike can cause pain, bleeding and distraction. A heavy blow can cause cartilage fracture and/or separation from the bone.

Nose (side of) – A moderate strike can cause pain, bleeding and possibly a nasal bone fracture.

Nose (under the) – A moderate strike can cause pain and distraction. A heavy blow can cause cartilage fracture and/or separation from the bone.

Radius Bone – A strike to this area can result in numbness to the hand or broken bones.

Preparing to Defend

Septum- The cartilage wall separating the nostrils of the nose is the septum. A strike to this area can result in extreme pain, bleeding and disorientation.

Shin – A moderate strike can cause bruising and pain, while a heavy strike can result in a fracture or inability to walk.

Skull (base of) – A moderate strike will cause pain and a headache. A strike to this area can cause disorientation. Unconsciousness has been known to result when strikes to the skull cause a shock that shakes the brain. Also, a strike that dislodges the vertebra could result in a fracture of the spinal cord.

Solar Plexus – A moderate strike to this area can disrupt breathing. This effect is commonly known as "knocking the wind out" of someone. A heavy strike can result in unconsciousness or cause internal organ damage.

Teeth (front of) – A strike to this area can result in broken bones and disorientation.

Temple – A strike to this area can result in disorientation or unconsciousness.

Thigh (inner, outer or back) – A strike to this area can result in muscular damage, cramping or numbness in the lower leg. This effect is commonly known a creating a painful "Charlie Horse."

Throat Hollow (Trachea) – The trachea, or throat hollow, is sensitive and vulnerable. Strikes to this area can result in serious injury or death.

Preparing to Defend

Wrist – A heavy blow can cause a bone injury. However, trapping the wrist and applying pressure can break the joint by hyperextending it. Trapping the wrist creates a "goose neck" and causes excruciating pain.

Preparing to Defend

Understanding Chokes

There are three basic ways of choking or strangling an opponent in the martial arts. Several techniques employ a combination of the three to induce an opponent's or an attacker's compliance. Because of the proven effectiveness of the chokes used in the martial arts, the techniques are explored in my self-defense sessions and introduced here. Study the information below and review the accompanying graphic of the human anatomy on page 35.

- Compress the carotid arteries on one or both sides of the neck to restrict the flow of blood and oxygen to the brain.
- Compress the trachea, also called the wind pipe, to stop or reduce the flow of air to the lungs.
- Compress the chest and lungs to prevent an opponent from inhaling. This choke is often used during pinning techniques.

These methods are sometimes referenced by various terms. They may be referred to as choking, strangling, head locks, or neck locks. In Judo these methods are grouped as a class of grappling techniques called *shime waza*. *Shime* means constriction and *waza* means technique; this group of techniques involves constriction.

In many martial arts a distinction is made between strangulation and choking. In context, the term strangulation refers to interfering with the flow of blood and oxygen to the brain. Choking refers to interfering with air

Preparing to Defend

passage to the larynx or trachea. Depending on the particular technique, one or several of these typically occur in combination.

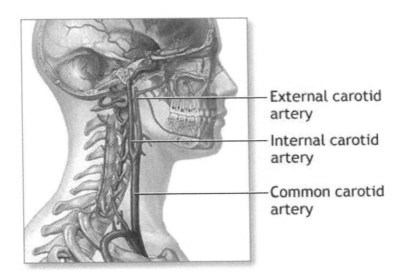

External carotid artery

Internal carotid artery

Common carotid artery

Compression of the carotid arteries is a preferred method for executing a controlled hold because it focuses on effortless power, as compared to powerful effort. This is what allows a smaller woman to subdue a larger, stronger attacker.

Preparing to Defend

It is important to understand when someone grabs your neck they may be exhibiting deadly intent.

Medical tests have established that the amount of pressure needed to occlude the arteries is six times less than the pressure needed to collapse the airway.[3]

Directly stopping the blood supply to the brain also results in loss of consciousness about six times faster than indirectly reducing oxygen to the brain through restricting breathing or the flow of air to the lungs.

If you are on the wrong side of the choke, time is at a premium when it comes to executing your countermeasures.

---

[3] Source: Principles of Judo Choking Techniques – "Different Chokes for Different Folks" by Neil Ohlenkamp, Revised January 1, 2005

Preparing to Defend

Managing the Controlled Hold

A properly executed controlled hold can cause unconsciousness within seconds. It should be used only under extreme conditions. The controlled hold is reviewed in this chapter because it is an effective defense method to down a predator when alternatives are limited. Within the context of self defense, this method's primary purpose is to create an escape opportunity. You should seek training from a self- defense professional before attempting the controlled hold for any reason. The controlled hold is an extreme tactic for an extreme circumstance. Therefore, it's important to understand guiding principles:

- Learn to understand the physiology of choking. Only a small amount of pressure is needed to cause unconsciousness.
- Learn to recognize the state of unconsciousness and to release the pressure immediately.
- Learn resuscitation methods.
- Avoid placing unconscious or restrained persons face down, this helps prevent them from choking on their own vomit. Keep an unconscious individual under observation until help arrives.

Preparing to Defend

The Recovery Position

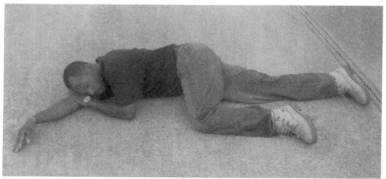

(The Recovery Position)

Study the photograph above, this gentleman is in a recovery position. All forms of the recovery position share basic principles. The mouth is downward so that fluid can drain from the airway; the chin is well up to keep the epiglottis open. Arms and legs are locked to stabilize the position of the individual.

If you recognize the state of unconsciousness and need to help an unconscious person recover, it is important to understand these guiding principles:

- Open the airway by putting one hand on the forehead and two fingers of the other hand on the chin of the unconscious person and gently tilt her/his head back to ensure the airway is open.
- Roll the person onto her/his side.

Preparing to Defend

Review the recovery position photo on page 38 along with these instructions:

- The hand on the patient's top arm is placed under his head to help keep the head elevated and the mouth open with the mouth downward.
- With a handcuffed or bound individual the hands will be placed behind his back, however the head is still elevated and the mouth open with the mouth downward.
- Adjust the legs to ensure the body stays in a stable position. The leg closest to you is often placed at 90 degrees.
- The recovery position is designed to help promote breathing as the patient's airway remains open. The position is also intended to keep the patient stable so that he won't roll onto his back.
- If the patient does not regain consciousness shortly, check to see whether he is breathing and has a pulse. If a pulse is detected just monitor him.
- If a patient is under the influence of any drugs or alcohol, he might not readily come around. If he fails either the breathing or pulse check, CPR is warranted and should be initiated. Initiate a 911 medical call quickly.

Preparing to Defend

If you are on the wrong side of the choke, time is at a premium when it comes to executing your countermeasures!

Chapter 3
Anti-Kidnapping Considerations

Most people who get taken away don't make it back!

Anti-Kidnapping Considerations

Loved and Not Forgotten

The tragic cases of Natalee Holloway and Laci Peterson are reminders that very bad things can happen to extremely good people. I suspect these women had something in common with women in my world. I imagine each embraced life and looked forward to the future with loving families and friends. Six days after Natalee Holloway graduated from high school in Alabama she was vacationing in the island country of Aruba. In the case of Laci Peterson, she was 7 months pregnant after hoping for years to conceive. In an instant, life revised the script for the families of these ladies. Natalee was abducted on the island and never seen again. Laci went missing for over a year until her remains and those of her fetus washed ashore in San Francisco Bay.

I am sickened when I think about Ms. Holloway, Ms. Peterson, and countless other women who have fallen victim to abduction. Since you are reading this book, I imagine you share my belief that personal safety is a component of a healthy existence. Crimes such as home invasions, workplace violence, and abductions scar entire families. The lesson that is reinforced each time I become aware of another Natalee or Laci situation: Daughters, sisters, mothers, wives and other women we love need dependable personal safety strategies. Encourage them to consistently practice self-defense skills. This chapter gives particular attention to strategies that may reduce one's risk of becoming the victim of abduction.

Anti-Kidnapping Considerations

Avoiding an Abduction

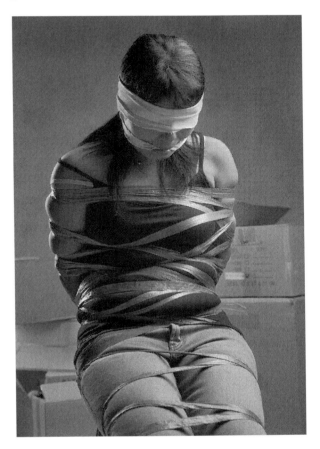

Kidnappings occur all over the world and for all sorts of reasons. Profiles of abductors range from family members, to sexual predators, to disgruntled employees, to ransom seekers.

Anti-Kidnapping Considerations

What is immediately clear is that there is no typical abduction, and as more people travel throughout the world, the often quoted advice to always fight your abductor may not be sage. On rare occasions, it may be best to cooperate or to feign cooperation. Sometime the situation may afford the opportunity for an immediate escape. A tactical escape beats a tactical encounter every time. Be prepared to think fast and act decisively.

Here are some safety tips:

1. Prepare for your safety: If you're walking in a public place, always be aware of who's around. Be attentive; make it a habit to spot an escape route every time you enter a new environment. Avoid dark alleys and parking lots, and/or get an escort. Lock your windows and doors day or night. Carry a cell phone and some personal safety devices (pepper spray, stun gun, ASP baton, use your keys as improvised weapons). Seriously consider getting a handgun and training and apply for a concealed carry weapons permit. Learn more about selecting a handgun by picking up a copy of my book "Defensive Handgun - Preparing to Prevail" by Mark James or visit my website at www.pantherprotectionservices.com.

2. Look Local: If you are traveling abroad, carry a newspaper or magazine printed in the local language. Even if you can't read it, no one knows that but you. Avoid wearing clothes that identify you as an outsider. Arrange for taxis through your hotel concierge desk. Read travel

Anti-Kidnapping Considerations

precautions on the US State Department or Department of Homeland Security website.

3. Follow your gut instinct. If it doesn't feel right it probably isn't right.

4. Vary your routes and times. Make it hard for attackers to anticipate your plans. Learn multiple ways to go between your home, office and any other location you routinely frequent.

5. Develop a plan. Prepare by assessing your situation before something bad happens. What kind of abduction would you be most likely to encounter? What will you do if someone attempts to kidnap you?

Rehearse possible scenarios, and be ready to act instantly should you actually be attacked. Most attackers are looking to catch you off guard, so having a plan shifts the element of surprise back in your favor. Know where the embassy of your home country is located when traveling abroad.

Often the best time to escape is at the onslaught of an abduction, as you are more familiar with those surroundings than if you are taken away to a remote location.

6. Dealing with multiple armed attackers: If they are seeking ransom and attempt to abduct you in an isolated or hostile place where there is realistically little to no chance of escape, you should probably cooperate with them from the start. A ransom hunter's major objective is often not to kill

Anti-Kidnapping Considerations

his hostage. This is frequently the case in parts of South America or Mexico for example, where well-organized kidnappers abduct business people for profit.

Express Kidnappings often occur as the kidnapper attempts to extort small sums of money quickly from tourists. The majority of people abducted in this manner are released alive. You are typically not as valuable to a ransom seeker if you are dead.

7. If you are thrown in the trunk, be aware most trunks have inside release levers. If the abductor is a professional predator, he may have disabled the trunk release latch. We will explore the trunk more in *"Understanding and Navigating the Trunk"* in the following pages.

8. If an abductor is unarmed, and it appears the attempt is sexually motivated, and if you are in the vicinity of other people, you should fight or do anything you can to escape.

9. Run away: If you've made the quick decision to run away, seek a safe public place while screaming for help. Don't stop until you've reached safety.

10. Put something between you and the attacker. You may not have the speed to out-run your attacker, but if you put something between you and him, you may be able to delay him long enough to get away, get others to come to your aid, or to cause him to give up. It may be a busy street; a group of people; even a car which you can run around as he tries to pursue you.

Anti-Kidnapping Considerations

11. Make a big scene: Scream, yell, run into innocent bystanders. Attract as much attention as possible to yourself and your attacker. Scream at the top of your lungs, attempt to attract others. For children, who may be less able to fight or flee an abductor, involving others may be their best chance of escape. Children should be taught to yell, "I'm being kidnapped!" or "Someone is trying to hurt my mommy!" Attempt to yell out the circumstances and a description of the attacker:

"A man with a knife is chasing me!"

"He's wearing a black shirt and light blue jeans!"

"I don't know this man!"

If innocent bystanders are not able to stop the abduction, they may at least be good witnesses.

12. Fight as if your life depends on it because it just might. Do whatever you need to get away. Use improvised weapons (keys to the eyes, ink pen to the eyes or throat, stick, rock). Attack the attacker's vitals (eyes, nose, throat, solar plexus, groin etc.).

Your goal is to stop the attack and get away, not beat the brakes off the attacker.

Anti-Kidnapping Considerations

13. Call 911. If you are subdued and able to conceal your cell phone immediately 911. It is best to call the police, but if you cannot, make the attacker feel that the police are on the way. "I dialed the panic button on my phone, just leave now and you won't be arrested."

Anti-Kidnapping Considerations

14. If you have observed someone following you, but you don't feel threatened by that individual, making direct eye contact often causes perpetrators to turn and leave. Even though you don't feel threatened remember, anyone who is following you is a threat.

Anti-Kidnapping Considerations

Understanding and Navigating the Trunk

At all cost try to avoid being placed into the trunk of a vehicle. Your compliance should not be an option in this situation! People who are abducted, placed in the trunk of a vehicle and driven away are often killed or never found. Because of the usually dire outcomes, this chapter helps you prepare a pre-fight bag as a self-defense tool. If faced with the trauma of being forced into the trunk of your own car your pre-fight bag may make the difference between life and death.

You are better off fighting than complying if you are in a highly populated area. There is a good chance someone may hear your screams, come to your aid or if you are injured a greater likelihood medical assistance can get to your aid quicker.

If you are forced into the trunk or back hatch consider these actions:

Anti-Kidnapping Considerations

- Try to remain calm.
- Listen to the sounds of the environment to help assess your whereabouts. Passing the information on to a 911 operator may help law officers find you. Understanding your whereabouts may also clue you to options for an escape route or objects to serve as improvised weapons.
- If you have a GPS feature on your cell phone and your phone has not been taken, try to activate it while you dial 911 from the trunk.
- If you are confined in your own trunk locate your emergency pre-staged fight bag. It was positioned in an inconspicuous, but accessible place. It contains:
  -small strong flashlight
  -folding knife
  -defensive and/or distraction countermeasures such as pepper spray, stun gun, or taser.

Anti-Kidnapping Considerations

- Use your flashlight to see the location of the trunk release latch or button while you are confined in your trunk.

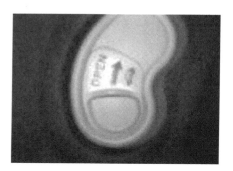

- The pocket knife in your pre-fight bag is designed to cut bonds, rope, or tape an attacker may have placed around you. If he has disabled the button or latch, try to locate the cable underneath the trunk carpet and operate it manually.
- The pepper spray, stun gun, taser and/or pocket knife are designed to aid in your self-defense and escape.
- Another option is to remove the tail light compartment and break the tail lights from the inside of the trunk. Through the opening you created, extend your hand to wave or another item to attract attention. Someone following the car may recognize a crime in progress, or the police may stop the vehicle. If you cannot breakout the tail lights, look to disconnect the wires to the tail lights.

Anti-Kidnapping Considerations

Practice escaping from a trunk using the tools in your pre-fight bag. From the safety of your own home, give someone you fully trust a set of keys to your trunk. Have him/her lock you in your car trunk. This will allow you to become familiar with being enclosed in a trunk. Rehearse moving around and finding your fight tools and bag. This will help you manage anxiety if you were involuntarily thrown in a trunk. If you are claustrophobic and your rear seats let down, practice moving around in the trunk with your seat(s) down to reduce your anxiety.

Before entering your trunk for this practice exercise, impose a limit on the time you are confined to ensure ample oxygen is available while you're inside.

Squeezing into a trunk will never be comfortable. However, familiarity with navigating your body inside a trunk will give you important tools for your defense arsenal. With practice you will learn to manage stress associated with being in a confined space or in a dark area. You can discover items that are common to the anatomy of any trunk and can serve as improvised weapons. Practice can help develop the state of calm needed to think clearly and strategize your counter attack. Staying calm may be the most important tool of all for someone forced into the trunk of a vehicle.

Anti-Kidnapping Considerations

Often the best time to escape is at the onslaught of an abduction, as you are often more familiar with those surroundings than if you are taken away to a remote location.

Chapter 4
Defense against Strikes

Spontaneous combustion doesn't just happen, you got to light yourself on fire!

Defense against Strikes

Ruckus in the Restaurant

The news media is replete with stories similar to one reported in Morrow, Georgia. Outside of a Cracker Barrel restaurant a man beat Army reservist Tasha Hill while her 7 year old child watched. The reservist was entering the restaurant as the man was leaving. Like a responsible parent would, Hill asked him to be careful of the restaurant's swinging door hitting her child. Apparently, things went downhill from there. Hill said the man slung open the door pretty hard and fast, which caused her to push her child out of the way. "I turned to the man and I just said, 'Excuse me sir, you need to watch yourself you almost hit my daughter in the face.' " said Hill. Witnesses reported to the police that the man threw the reservist to the ground and hit her head with his fists and feet.

All over the country people like Ms. Hill wake up and look forward to embracing life and sharing simple joys with loved ones. Yet, bullies and other assailants pass through Everytown U.S.A. on their way to stealing our peace. They dine among us. They work with us. They live among us. They date us and marry us. They prey on people who appear to be easy targets. Self defense training helps *us* to more quickly recognize *them* so threats are reduced. Training is important for ingraining defensive tactics and increasing situational awareness. This chapter of *Common Sense Self-Defense* is dedicated to defending against strikes as a strategy for increasing the odds of walking away safely from unexpected encounters such as Ms. Hill's.

Defense against Strikes

Blocking a Hook or Circular Punch

Defense against Strikes

- Your reaction hand closest to the adversary's hook punch blocks out and up.
- Whole body needs to turn (to supply power and reduce the impact of the blow).
- Reaction hand stays inside of adversary's hand/arm, which allows you to launch a counter attack to the adversary's eyes, nose, or throat.
- Off hand is held approximately chest high to react to the adversary's other hand should they launch an attack. On page 57 Lana executes a hammer fist to the nose followed by a series of elbows.
- Run away!

Reaction Hand is the hand that initially responds (either consciously or subconsciously) by blocking, striking, countering or defending.

Off Hand is the non initiating hand and often used for covering, launching a counter attack, or to provide additional defense should the reaction hand fail in executing the initial move.

Hammer Fist is a striking technique where you use the lower pad of the palm below your little finger of a clinched fist as your point of impact. You point at your target with your elbow to line up your hammer fist strike. The power is delivered by transferring your weight through your shoulder down your bent arm into the fist. The most effective targets are the collar bone, bridge of the nose, lip or groin.

Defense against Strikes

Blocking a Straight Punch (outside block)

Defense against Strikes

- Simultaneously as you are turning off the line of attack, reaction hand closest to the adversary's punch blocks across on the adversary's elbow.
- Reaction hand stays outside of adversary's hand/arm which allows you to launch a counter attack over the top.
- Off hand is held approximately chest high to react to the adversary's other hand should he launch an attack. Alternatively, your off hand can be used to catch/cover adversary's initial strike should it pass through your initial block. In the photo on page 59, Lana delivers a palm heel strike to the chin followed by an elbow to the adversary's ear and temple.
- Run away!

Defense against Strikes

Blocking a Straight Punch (inside block)

Defense against Strikes

- Simultaneously as you are turning off the line of attack, reaction hand closest to the adversary's straight punch blocks out and up.
- Your whole body needs to turn to supply power. This is particularly important when fighting a bigger adversary.
- Reaction hand stays inside of adversary's hand/arm which allows you to launch a counter attack to adversary's eyes, nose, throat or other vital area.
- Your off hand is held approximately chest high to react to adversary's other hand should he launch an attack. Alternatively, your off hand held chest high to deflect the punch if it passes through.
- In the photo on page 61, Lana launches a counter strike with her off hand followed by a knee to the face.
- Run away!

Defense against Strikes

Blocking an Uppercut

Defense against Strikes

- Simultaneously as you are stepping off the line of attack, reaction hand closest to the adversary's uppercut blocks down against the inside of the attacker's forearm.
- Reaction hand stays inside of adversary's hand/arm which allows you to launch a counter attack if required to adversary's eyes, nose, throat or other vital areas.
- In the photo on page 63, Lana launches a back fist to the throat of her adversary. Followed by a knee to the groin.
- Off hand is held approximately chest high to react to adversary's other hand should he launch an attack.
- Run away!

Chapter 5
Defense against Grabs

If it doesn't have to be a fight, let's not make it be a fight. But if we have to fight, we fight ferociously!

Defense against Grabs

Nasty Neighbor

For nearly a year and a half my buddy's daughter had been experiencing some very inconsiderate behavior from a neighbor. Her neighbor, we will call him John instead of one of the nasty names he calls women, had a habit of playing music incredibly loud during all hours of the day and night. One day, my buddy's daughter saw her neighbor in the parking lot. Assuming that he simply did not realize his volume disturbed the peace of others, she innocently asked him if he could possibly be a little more considerate and not play his music so loudly late into the night. She explained that she is a student and the loud music breaks her concentration during study time. To give perspective on what happened next, understand that my buddy's slender daughter is 5'5" tall and weighs 115 pounds. The muscular neighbor is approximately 6'2" tall at 220 pounds.

In response, the neighbor proceeded to berate the young woman. My grandmother would say the guy "went to town" with behavior totally void of home training! He called her the b-word*!@ and used some very choice disgusting terms. He offered up a few racial slurs and closed his vocal performance saying he would play his music how he wanted and whenever he wanted. The young woman left the scene feeling intimated and vulnerable to the neighbor's threatening conduct.

For months the young woman continued to suffer through his loud music and checked to see whether the parking lot was clear of him before leaving her condo. Then one day it

Defense against Grabs

hit the proverbial fan. My buddy was at his daughter's condo repairing a leaking faucet when the neighbor began to play his music loudly. On this occasion my buddy employed condo etiquette, tapping on the floor as a signal to turn the music down. The loud music continued while his daughter recounted her horrific encounter with the neighbor. Her narration was interrupted by an aggressive knock on the door. My buddy opened it, and in the doorway stood a man who fit the disturbing description. He asked "Are you John from downstairs?" When John responded affirmatively, the young woman witnessed a good lesson on "put something hard on something soft."

I am extremely glad her dad happened to be there on that occasion. Who knows what would have transpired had his daughter been there alone.

Defense against Grabs

Wrist Grab Releases

Basic Wrist Grab

Defense against Grabs

Please see photos page 68 for Lana's demonstration of the following:

- Rotate your wrist toward the attacker's thumb and forefinger applying pressure toward the thumb and forefinger.
- This move is similar to the technique for blocking a hook or circular punch.
- Strike with the off hand to the most assessable vital areas.
- Run away!

Defense against Grabs

Cross Wrist Grab

- Rotate your wrist toward the attacker's thumb (this is the weakest part of their grip) and forefinger, applying pressure toward the thumb and forefinger.
- Strike with the off hand to the most accessible vital areas.
- If you get stuck, hyperextend the attacker's arm and strike hard directly on the elbow.

- Run away!

Defense against Grabs

Alternate Technique

Defense against Grabs

- On page 71 as the attacker attempts to pull Lana towards him she doesn't resist. She uses the attacker's momentum against him.
- As she steps in, the purpose of her initial downward strike (to the top of the attacker's forearm) is to break the grab.
- She then follows with two elbows to the face and throat area.
- Run away!

Defense against Grabs

Defending a Double Handed Push

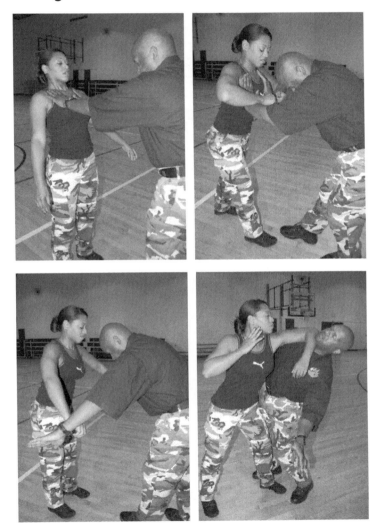

Defense against Grabs

- Slap the attackers hands down as Lana demonstrates on page 73.
- Followed by an elbow to the throat, face, solar plexus or other vital area.
- Followed by a knee to the face or groin
- Run away!

Defense against Grabs

Defending a Ponytail Grab

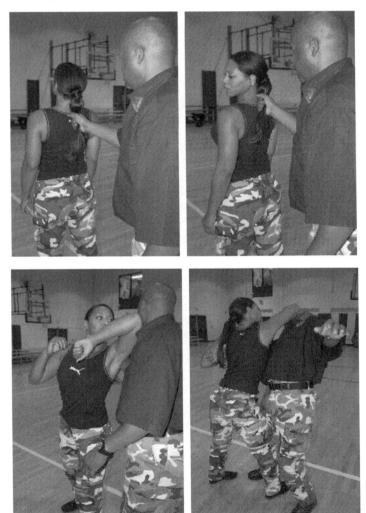

Defense against Grabs

- Turn your head toward the direction of the attacker to release the pressure of the grab.
- Strike to most accessible vital area:
  -Ridge hand to throat
  -Punch to solar plexus
  -Palm heel strike to the bridge of nose or other vital area.
- In the photos on page 75 Lana turns and delivers two elbows to the face.
- Run away!

Chapter 6
Defense against Holds

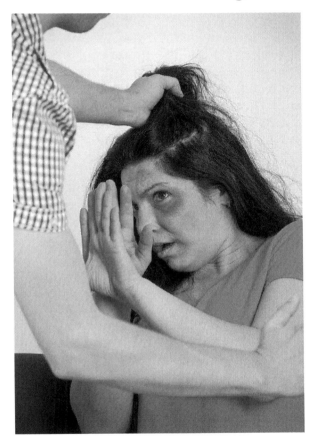

Injuries are what stop a motivated attacker and allow us to prevail against bigger, faster, stronger attackers.

Defense against Holds

Rough First Day

According to an article in the Atlanta Journal Constitution, an elementary school principal suffered a broken arm after being robbed on the first day of school. Rita Harper-Hastings was attacked around 6:45 a.m. as she was getting out of her car at Stone Mill Elementary School in Stone Mountain, Georgia. The principal reported that the suspect struck her before fleeing with her purse, cell phone and wallet. The woman's injuries required treatment for a broken arm, bump on the head and several bruises. After being released from a medical center she missed additional days from work recovering.

In the meantime, police officers searched the area looking for the teenager suspected of perpetrating the attack in the parking lot. The suspect was found wreaking another kind of mayhem. Apparently, the suspect was attempting to break into a neighborhood home. The juvenile was charged with aggravated battery, robbery by force and burglary.

The incident triggered safety concerns for adults and young children at the school. A deputy chief superintendent said a school resource officer would be assigned the elementary school. The district also sent a letter to parents about the robbery and distributed safety tips to all school employees.

The assault and following home invasion occurred during the light of day in a typical suburban neighborhood. Surely, both incidents left innocent parties questioning what defensive measures might have helped.

Defense against Holds

Full Nelson

Defense against Holds

- Reach up and grab one of the attacker's fingers as Lana demonstrates on page 79 and hyperextend or break it - try for two or as many as possible.
- Once you grab the fingers execute a butt bump to create space and further weaken the attacker's grip. Then step to the side and out of the attacker's grasp while maintaining the pressure on the hand and fingers of the attacker as you force the attacker to the ground.
- Run away!

Defense against Holds

Defending a Bear Hug from the Rear (attacker is close)

Defense against Holds

- Spread your feet outside of your shoulders, and stoop to lower your body's center of gravity as Lana demonstrates on page 81. This position is called the horse stance and makes one's body more difficult to lift.
- Aggressively lean forward and execute the butt bump; this helps create space.
- Aggressively shift your hips to the side, this opens up the attacker's groin area and solar plexus.
- Followed by an elbow to throat or solar plexus.
- Followed by a hammer fist to the groin.
- May be followed by repeated knee strikes to groin or solar plexus.
- Run away!

The horse stance is the beginning of your attack against the attacker. This stance can help prevent you from being carried away and potentially kidnapped.

When you are in a familiar environment you have the advantage of knowing where things are located, which maximizes your strategic options. At home you know where your weapons are located. At your office you know the route to the security guard station. When you are taken to an unfamiliar place, everything changes. As a first objective do not get carried away, literally.

Defense against Holds

Alternate Technique

Defense against Holds

Please see photos on page 83 for Lana's demonstration of the following:

- Instep Stomp.
- Butt bump.
- Elbow to the solar plexus.
- Hammer fist to the groin.
- Elbow to the head.
- Run away!

Defense against Holds

Defending a Bear Hug from the Front (your arms on top)

Defense against Holds

- Grab the attacker by the back of the head and insert both thumbs into the attacker's eyes as Lana demonstrates on page 85.
- Followed by palm heel strikes to the ears (like you are in the band clapping a pair of cymbals)
- Followed by an elbow to the face or throat and repeated knee strikes to the groin.
- Run away!

Defense against Holds

Alternate Technique (your arms below)

Defense against Holds

Please see photos on page 87 for Lana's demonstration of the following:

- Reach up and drive your palm heels into the sides of the attacker while simultaneously grabbing the flesh of the attacker's side.
- Execute the love handle grab.
- Followed by repeated knee strikes to the groin.
- Run away!

Defense against Holds

Defending an attack from the Rear against a Car or Wall (attacker holding your hands)

Defense against Holds

- Absorb the impact of the wall with your forearms making sure you turn your head to the side so you don't strike the wall face first as Lana demonstrates on page 89.
- If you feel the attacker's head is close to you, consider head butting to the nose.
- If the attacker's hips are close to you consider butt bumping the attacker to help create space. Butt bumping the attacker hard also has the effect of simultaneously weakening the grip on your arms.
- Lift up your foot and execute mule kick to the knee or shin or you may execute an instep stomp.
- With all your body weight turn and elbow attacker in the solar plexus or face.
- Strike, poke or rake to the eyes.
- Run away!

Mule kick is a striking technique which resembles the swift kick of a mule. To execute raise your foot up under you and toward the rear, bending your body downward from the waist. Aggressively thrust your foot to the rear using the arch as the striking point. This strike is typically targeted toward an attacker's shin or knee.

Defense against Holds

Alternate Technique

Defense against Holds

- Absorb the impact of the wall with your forearms making sure you turn your head to the side so you don't strike the wall face first as Lana demonstrates on page 91.
- Simultaneously as you turn toward the attacker raise one of your arms above the attacker's outstretched arms and armbar both of the attacker's arms.
- With all your body weight turn and elbow attacker in the solar plexus or face.
- Follow up by repeated knee strikes to the groin or face.
- Run away!

Defense against Holds

Defending an Attack from the Rear against a Car (attacker holding neck or shoulders)

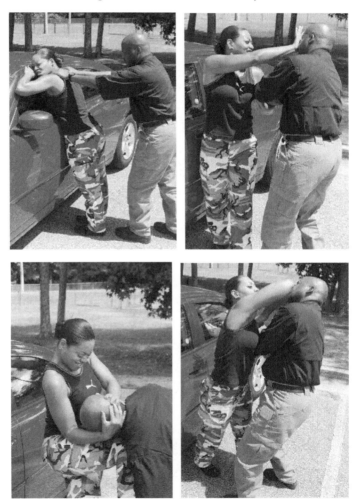

Defense against Holds

Please see photos on page 93 for Lana's demonstration of the following:

- Absorb the impact of the wall with your forearms making sure you turn your head to the side so you don't strike the car face first.
- Raise one arm high while turning into the attacker (make sure you clear the attacker's wrist) and armbar both of his arms.
- Other arm continues the turn while poking or raking at the attacker's eyes, in the photo on page 93 Lana executes a palm heel strike to the attacker's nose.
- May be followed by repeated knee strikes to the face or groin and additional elbows.
- Run away!

Defense against Holds

Defending the Over the Shoulder Grab (Date Hug Defense)

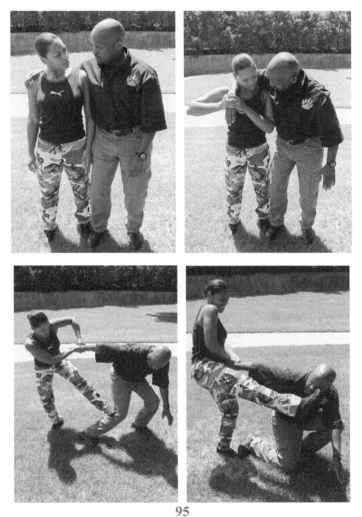

Defense against Holds

This defense is useful when what starts out as a hand on your shoulder progresses to a breast grab.

- Initially reach up softly and grab control of the attacker's hand and arm, as if you are welcoming the advance. This is a ploy on your part as we are softening up the attacker for our counter move.
- Now squeeze and control the attacker's wrist and hand as you spin your hips out and away from the attacker as Lana demonstrates on page 95.
- Left leg kicks attacker's knee taking the attacker down.
- Right leg executes a kick to the face.
- Run away!

Defense against Holds

Alternate Technique (attacker pulling you in – your left arm in the front of the attacker)

Defense against Holds

- When your left arm is in front of the attacker, execute a back fist to the groin as Lana demonstrates on page 97.
- Followed by a hammer fist under the chin with your left arm.
- Right hand follows up with an open hand strike to the throat.
- Run away!

Defense against Holds

Alternate Technique (attacker pulling you in – your left arm behind the attacker)

Defense against Holds

Please see photos on page 99 for Lana's demonstration of the following:

- Reach up with your left arm and hand from the rear and grab the attacker's chin and aggressively turn the attacker's head to the left.
- Right hand follows with an open hand strike to the throat.
- Follow with a hammer fist to the groin.
- Run away!

Defense against Holds

Alternate Technique (attacker pulling you in – your left arm behind the attacker)

Defense against Holds

- Turn your head to the left and look at the attacker as Lana demonstrates on page 101.
- Right hand strikes to the attacker's eyes.
- Left arm and hand from the rear reaches up and grabs the attacker's chin and aggressively turns the attacker's head to the left.
- Right hand follows with an open hand strike to the throat.
- Run away!

Defense against Holds

Alternate Technique (attacker pulling you in – your left arm behind the attacker)

Defense against Holds

- Turn your head to the left and look at the attacker as Lana demonstrates on page 103.
- Right hand strikes to the attacker's eyes.
- Left hand from the rear reaches up and grabs the back of the attacker's collar and aggressively pulls the attacker's head straight back and down.
- Right hand follows up with an open hand strike to the throat.
- Run away!

Defense against Holds

Defending a Bull Rush

Defense against Holds

- As the attacker starts coming forward drop one foot back to maintain your balance as Lana demonstrates on page 105.

- Grab the attacker's head by placing one hand below his chin and the other hand on or near his ear.

- Rotate his head. Where the head goes the body will follow. Be extremely careful when executing this technique as it is very easy to break someone's neck if done aggressively.
- Run away!

Chapter 7
Defense against Chokes

All violent acts are the same. There is a person committing violence and a person receiving a violent act!

Defense against Chokes

Wow in Wal-Mart

An incident involving a mother and her young daughter left women appalled throughout Georgia. After hearing the story reported by CBS, one of my business associates summed her emotional reaction saying, "Wow, it's shuttering to know somebody would do that to a kid!"

A woman named Sonja Mathews was in an Atlanta area Wal-Mart with her child when the disturbing event happened. According to the news, her two year old was slapped in the face by 61 year old Roger Stephens after he became angry about the young girl's crying. Ms. Mathews said the man warned, "If you don't shut her up, I'll do it for you." After she failed to quiet the child, Stephens slapped the youngster several times in the face. He was quoted as saying, "See, I told you I would shut her up."

The woman screamed at the assailant and cried for help. Another shopper interceded and stopped the assault. Store security also showed up before the child suffered serious injury. Fortunately, the child's injuries were limited to some redness in the face. She was treated and released at the scene. Ms. Mathews said she had the impression that the assailant was mentally ill. Stephens was later convicted and served jail time for child cruelty.

When it comes to our children our vulnerability is exposed. This is why it is important to seek professional training and learn to become your own first line of defense.

Defense against Chokes

Single Hand Choke

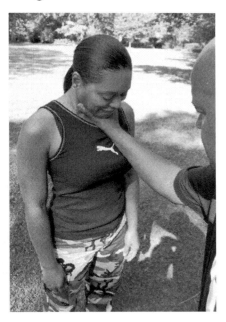

- Any time you are being choked, the first thing to do is try to take the pressure off the choke.
- The moment you feel a hand on your throat immediately attempt to drop your chin into your chest.
- Your chin will come to rest in the crevice between your attacker's thumb and index finger.

Defense against Chokes

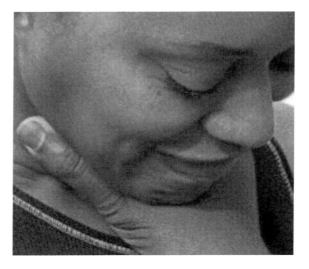

- Use your chin to apply pressure to the attacker's hand. To execute this move imagine you are trying to bury your chin in your chest.
- Applying pressure on the attacker's hand will minimize or restrict his ability to close his fingers and choke you.
- While this position is uncomfortable you are still able to breathe and most importantly fight!

Defense against Chokes

Front Naked Choke

Defense against Chokes

- Bring your hands together in the praying position and bring your hands up through the attacker's arms.
- Your hands come under and through the attacker's arms verses over the top of them.
- Your right hand grabs the back of the attacker's neck and your left index or middle finger knuckle is inserted underneath the attacker's chin positioned high on the throat against his trachea as Lana demonstrates on page 111.
- Apply direct pressure with both hands. This inflicts intense pain and will give the attacker the gag reflex.
- Keep applying pressure until the attacker drops to his knees.
- Run away!

Defense against Chokes

Alternate Technique

Defense against the Choke

- Two extended fingers thrust to his trachea.
- Implement this technique by coming under and through attacker's arms verses over the top of the attacker's arms; this helps hide your counter attack.
- Follow with a punch to the throat or solar plexus with your other hand.
- Kick to groin or knee to the groin.
- Run away!

Defense against Chokes

Alternate Technique

Defense against Chokes

Please see photos on page 114 for Lana's demonstration of the following:

- With your right hand reach over the top to the attacker's far hand that is around your throat. Your thumb is inserted into the web of the attacker's hand between his thumb and forefinger. With your remaining fingers grab the fatty part of the attacker's palm.
- While gripping the attacker's palm, rotate your right hand until your thumb exposes the attacker's palm and elbow toward the sky. This position should hyperextend the attacker's arm.
- By maintaining the steady pressure you should become free from the attacker's choke.
- With your other hand or forearm you may strike hard at the attacker's elbow to create an arm break.
- While maintaining control of the attacker's arm, you may also place a kick to the side of attacker's knee or shin to create a break. If you step on the back his calf or back of the knee you will push the attacker to the ground.

Defense against Chokes

Alternate Technique

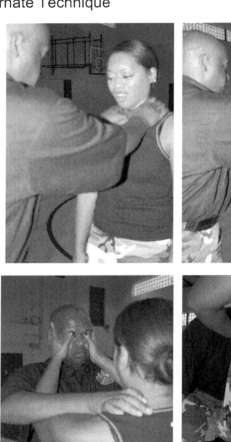

Defense against Chokes

Please see photos on page 116 for Lana's demonstration of the following:

- Your hands come up from below the attacker's arms as if praying or forming a pyramid.
- Hands proceed up through the attacker's arms and grab the attacker's head from the rear while inserting both thumbs into the attacker's eyes.
- Follow with repeated knee strikes to the face or groin.
- Run away!

Defense against Chokes

Rear Naked Choke

Defense against Chokes

Please see photos on page 118 for Lana's demonstration of the following:

- Turn your head toward the attacker's hands (toward the right in the picture).
- Hips turn aggressively outward in the opposite direction (toward the left in the picture). This position now provides access to the attacker's groin.
- Execute an elbow to the solar plexus, followed by a hammer fist to his groin.
- Run away!

Defense against Chokes

Alternate Technique for a Rear Choke or Side Headlock

Defense against Chokes

Please see photos on page 120 for Lana's demonstration of the following:

- Anytime someone attempts to choke you first try to drop your chin into chest to reduce the pressure of the choke. This helps reduce the pressure on the carotid artery and reduces the attacker's ability to choke you unconscious quickly.
- Turn your head toward the attacker's hands.
- Turn your hips aggressively outward the opposite direction and drop your left leg behind the attacker's right leg.
- Straighten your left arm and aggressively turn to the left throwing the attacker over your left leg.
- Run away!

Defense against Chokes

Defending a Headlock

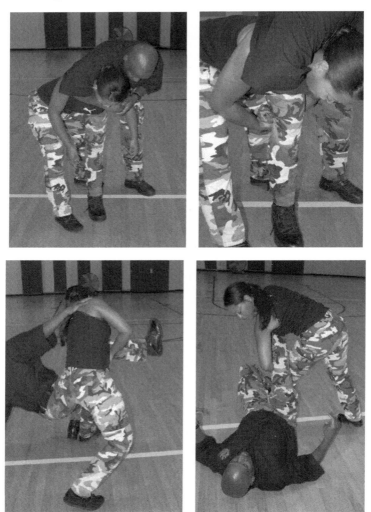

Defense against Chokes

Please see photos on page 122 for Lana's demonstration of the following:

- Anytime someone attempts to choke you first try to drop your chin into chest to reduce the pressure of the choke. This helps reduce the pressure on the carotid artery and reduces the attacker's ability to choke you unconscious quickly.
- Bend over and grab the attacker's leg with both of your arms.
- Lower your hips; this will lower your center of gravity. Use your back muscles to help lift the attacker's leg as you turn toward him.
- Use your left leg to sweep the attacker's left foot/ankle and throw him to the ground.
- Run away!

Defense against Chokes

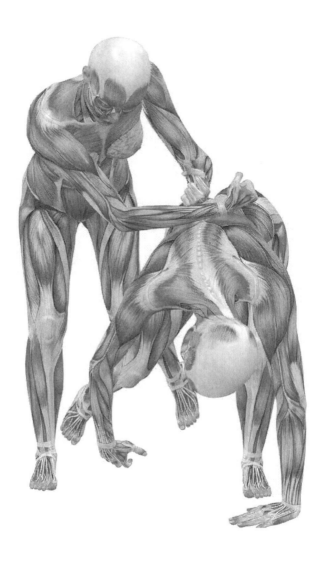

Chapter 8
Weapons Disarming

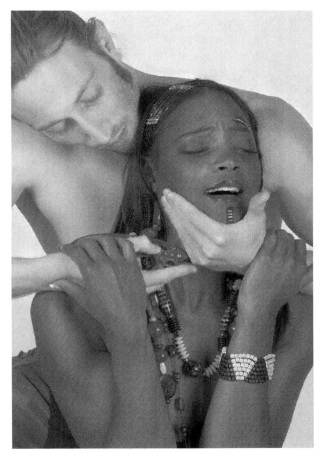

Hope is not a strategy!

Weapons Disarming

Terror on the Transit

Toni, who is evidence that age 40 really is the new 29, is now convinced that self defense training is important to having a grounded sense of safety. Her vulnerability stared her in the face last summer when she took her mother and 4 year old daughter on a routine trip to the mall via the local mass transit system. They traveled the same route they've navigated for years to the mall. The difference on that occasion was the interest taken in the threesome by a man who, as described by Toni, was clearly under the influence of alcohol.

Shopping bags in hand and 4 year old in tow, Toni and her mom tried to ignore his glances. Turning away did not remedy the situation. From her peripheral vision she saw the inebriated man advancing toward the family and all three heard the crass remarks hurdled at them. Thinking smartly, she whispered to her mom that they would exit the train immediately at the next stop. Fortunately, before the situation escalated they were able to get off at the next stop. Unlike the fairy tales there was no white knight in shining armor riding in to save the damsel in distress-- the other passengers just looked away seemingly relieved that the threat was not directed at them.

Toni is intelligent, tall, athletic and not easily intimidated so on most days she too might have simply looked away. But that day someone targeted her, intentionally trying to steal her joy and break her peace. She said she was 'thankful" that the family had avoided imminent danger.

Weapons Disarming

Toni says she didn't know at first what she could have done had she been forced into a physically violent encounter.

Being the woman she is, she made a conscious decision to increase her knowledge of personal safety techniques. I had the honor of consulting with her about proven self defense strategies. Toni still rides the mass transit system to handle her business and she isn't afraid to look good doing it.

Weapons Disarming

Defending a Stick or Bottle

Weapons Disarming

Please see photos on page 128 for Lana's demonstration of the following:

- As the attacker draws back the stick or bottle immediately step forward and insert your reaction arm (the one closet to the weapon) directly into the opening between the weapon and the attacker's face.
- With your reaction arm, wrap the attacker's arm creating an armbar of the attacker's weapon arm.
- Then with your other hand and knees attack his vitals.

Weapons Disarming

Weapon Disarm from Front

Weapons Disarming

When an assailant has a weapon there is generally a small window of opportunity to consider and execute your countermeasures. Therefore, you must be prepared to quickly execute your selected counter attack. On page 130 Lana demonstrates one option to effectively disarm the attacker.

Please see photos on page 130 for Lana's demonstration of the following:

- Start from the bargaining position (hands up and in front you in a non threatening position – hands open verses making a fist).
- Your left hand grabs attacker's hand and wrist, use your right hand to secure your grip.
- Position both of your thumbs just at the intersection of his hand and fingers, then aggressively turn attacker's hand outward. If done quickly, you will execute a throw.
- Depending on attacker's position, look to step aggressively onto the side of his knee or calf.
- Attacker should release the weapon, or at minimum you will create an opportunity to escape.
- Run away!

Weapons Disarming

Weapons Disarm from the Rear

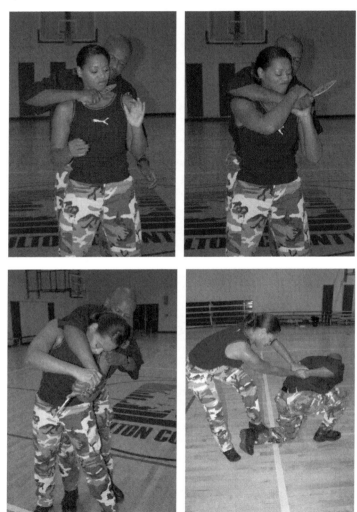

Weapons Disarming

Please see photos on page 132 for Lana's demonstration of the following:

- Take control of the knife hand and wrist. Hold it like your life depends on it, because it does.
- Execute the butt bump to create space between your body and his.
- As you control the knife, start turning the blade down, as you work to maintain the space created from the butt bump.
- As you continue to turn your hips outward look to armbar the attacker's knife hand behind his back. This helps you maintain control.
- If you find yourself at the back or side of the attacker execute a knee break by stepping on the side of his knee or ankle break by stepping down on his ankle.
- Run away!

An *armbar* is a joint lock used in various grappling martial arts that hyperextends the elbow joint. It is typically applied by placing the opponent's extended arm at the elbow over a fulcrum such as an arm, leg or hip, and controlling the opponent's body while leveraging the arm over the fulcrum.

Weapons Disarming

Alternate Technique

Weapons Disarming

Please see photos on page 134 for Lana's demonstration of the following:

- Take control of the knife hand and wrist. Hold it like your life depends on it, because it does.
- Execute the butt bump to create space between his body and yours.
- As you gain control the blade, start turning the blade up, which simultaneously rotates the attacker's palm to the sky. With the attacker's arm hyperextended (the attacker's elbow will be facing downward) over your shoulder apply continuous pressure downward until the attacker's arm breaks.
- Off side arm applies an elbow to the solar plexus.
- Hammer fist to the groin.
- Run away!

Weapons Disarming

Alternate Technique

Weapons Disarming

Please see photos on page 136 for Lana's demonstration of the following:

- Take control of the knife hand and wrist. Hold it like your life depends on it, because it does.
- Execute the butt bump to create space between his body and yours.
- As you work to control the knife, start turning the blade down. Maintain the space created by the butt bump by turning your hips out and away from the attacker.
- As you continue to turn your hips outward look to armbar the attacker's weapon hand behind him. Place the handle of the blade against your hips and drive your hips forward stabbing the attacker with his own knife.
- Run away!

Weapons Disarming

Females are generally murdered by people they know. In 64% of female homicide cases, females were killed by a family member or intimate partner. Keep the element of surprise on your side. Train hard and keep your skills development to yourself. It is an unfortunate reality that you may have to use your training on someone you know.

Chapter 9
Fighting from your Back

Just because you are on your back, it doesn't mean you are vulnerable. It just means you are on your back. Fight from where you are until you get to where you want to be!

Fighting from your Back

Gray Areas

Recently I talked with a woman in one of my women's self
defense classes. Respecting her privacy, I'll call her Olivia
for the purpose of sharing the experience that led her to
enroll in my training session. Olivia said she thinks of herself
as a strong, independent woman. She told me that friends
and family members comment on her self confidence; they
perceive her as level headed and smart when it comes to
decisions about men and relationships. In spite of her poise
and independence, Olivia was haunted by the memory of
something that occurred years ago — a sexual encounter
that left her wondering: *Was I raped?* According to Olivia,
she is less concerned today with the unanswered question.
Instead, she was participating in my training class to prevent
ever again having a sexual encounter that would fall into a
gray area. She intended to prevail the next time she said
"no" to sex with an acquaintance.

Here is what happened: Before Olivia enrolled in my training
sessions.   She had asked a co-worker, Bob, to be her
"platonic date" at a jazz festival. They joined others for
dinner first, and then everyone headed to the festival. She
remembers that she had quite a bit of alcohol that night and
admittedly was inebriated, but not what she would call
sloppy wasted.

After the jazz festival, they went to Bob's house and,
eventually, started heavy petting. She told him flat out that
she didn't want it to proceed to sex, and he said okay. But
within a few minutes, he had pushed her down on the sofa

Fighting from your Back

and positioned himself on top of her. "No. Stop," she said softly — too softly, she later told herself. When he disregarded her command and advanced anyway, she tensed up and tried to go numb until it was over. He fell asleep afterward. She pulled herself together and left his house "having this dirty feeling of not knowing whether it was my fault and whether to report it." While it felt like rape to her — she had not wanted to have sex with Bob — she was not sure if that's what anyone else would call it. Olivia said the incident fell into a gray area. "Maybe I wasn't forceful enough in saying I didn't want it." Even today, she is reluctant to call it rape because she does not view herself as weak or as a victim. Wisely, she decided to learn more about personal protection techniques that might have empowered her during a terribly weak moment.

Olivia's ambiguous experience has become so common it has earned its own terminology. The phrase "gray rape" was coined to refer to sex that falls somewhere between consent and denial. Identifying a gray rape is more difficult than date rape because often both parties are unsure of who wanted what. And it's a surprisingly common occurrence.

The U.S. Department of Justice estimates that 1 in 5 college women will be raped at some point during a five-year college career; approximately 9 out of 10 times the victim will know her assailant; and half of all victims will not call what happened rape. Sixty-two percent of female rape victims say they were assaulted by someone they knew, which includes dates, acquaintances, and random hookups.

Fighting from your Back

Many experts feel that gray rape is a consequence of today's hookup culture: lots of partying and flirting, plenty of alcohol, and ironically, the idea that women can be just as bold and adventurous about sex as men are. Living safely in this culture means women should become intimate with the self protection concepts explained in *Common Sense Self-Defense* and in my live training sessions.

Fighting from your Back

Defense against being Knocked Down (Attacker approaching straight in – Knee Break)

Fighting from your Back

- As you fall or get knocked to your back, tuck your chin into your chest (leaning your head forward) so your head doesn't strike the ground. Deliberately allow yourself to fall onto your buttocks. Falling back on your arms may break one or both of your arms.
- As the attacker continues approaching, hook the back of his heel with your heel so he can't pull away. Use your opposite foot to aggressively attack his knee, breaking his knee as Lana demonstrates on page 143. A hard strike below his knee to his shin will usually cause him to lose his balance and fall forward. A hard strike directly on the knee will typically cause a break.
- Get up and run away!

Fighting from your Back

Alternate Technique (Attacker approaching straight in – Leg Scissor)

Fighting from your Back

- As the attacker continues approaching, hook the back of the attacker's heel with one of your heels.
- As you aggressively roll onto your side, use your opposite foot to aggressively attack his knee as you continue rolling this will cause the attacker to fall away from you as Lana demonstrates on page 145.
- Get up and run away!

Fighting from your Back

Defending a Mount

Fighting from your Back

- Stay calm. Preserve your energy, and try to de-escalate the situation. It is not time to launch your counter attack yet.
- Remaining calm allows you to strategize your defense and helps you preserve the energy needed to attack the attacker.
- While the attacker is holding your hands he can't rape or assault you.
- If he is using both of his hands to hold you, he can't do anything else with them. He must release one of your hands to hit you, or go to his zipper, pocket or anything else.
- Once he releases one of your arms, attack his groin, then his throat as Lana demonstrates on page 147.
- Drive your knee into his tail bone.
- Get up and run away!

Fighting from your Back

Alternate Technique

 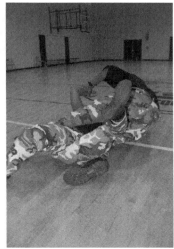

Fighting from your Back

- If the attacker tries to place his knees on your shoulders in an attempt to pin your arms, he will ease forward. Immediately before he places his knees on your shoulder, drive your knee into his tail bone, this will off-balance the attacker as Lana demonstrates on page 149.
- As the attacker falls forward rotate your hips to get from under the attacker.
- Get up and run away.

Fighting from your Back

Defending a Mount and Choke

Fighting from your Back

- Place your hands above your head and grab your elbows as Lana demonstrates on page 151.
- Aggressively bring your forearms down across your attacker's forearms. Pin his forearms to your chest and hold them tightly.
- Use your hips and legs to aggressively roll the attacker to either side. The attacker can't catch himself or break his fall because you are holding his arms and hands.
- Get up and run away!

Chapter 10
Improvised Weapons

Yep that will work.

Improvised Weapons

College Chaos

When my daughter was a sophomore in college, one of her good friends was asked out on a date that both the young women considered a dream date. My daughter's friend is a talented and outgoing young woman; at the time she envisioned her date with one of the university's star ball players as romantic and full of promise. The first string ball player had proposed an evening of dining at a popular college eatery, then hitting a couple of parties, and then quiet time so that the two could get to know each other. This was the grown up stuff that many young ladies dream of from the time they become cognizant of their femininity. My daughter and her good friend spent three days preparing her wardrobe. The perfect pair of jeans was coordinated with a blouse that complemented the stitching on the jean's pockets and piping. The just right handbag was matched with awesome shoes. The young ladies even practiced date dialog. "If he says this, I think I'll say that." When date night rolled around, the young lady innocently left her apartment with the athlete. She went off beautifully and appropriately dressed with a dream guy she credited with being fun, respectful and trustworthy.

Surprised that her good friend had not sent a single text message during the evening, the next day my daughter sent a text: "SUP" (What's up?). Her friend's response: "N2M" (Not too much). In following days her friend became conspicuously absent from activities she previously enjoyed. In class, the good friend seemed jittery. Exactly what happened during the dream date to cause the young

Improvised Weapons

woman's withdrawn behavior is unknown to us. However, one thing seems clear. In similar situations, withdrawing is often a coping mechanism used in an attempt to disassociate, hide or forget a traumatic experience. Did this young woman's dream date become her nightmare?

The experience afforded a teachable moment. My daughter and I discussed the additional preparation that is critical for *any* date to conclude with a young woman's dignity and physical well being intact. It is understandable that my daughter's friend invested time in glamorizing for her special occasion. I believe an equivalent investment should be made in preparing to prevail should an occasion turn ominous. It is normal for a woman to enhance the attributes that make her feel good about herself. Intelligence, attitude, humor, cosmetics, hair styling, and clothing are familiar tools in the female arsenal. I advised my daughter that intelligence is a particularly powerful tool- especially when the body of knowledge includes reliable self-defense strategies.

Healthy relationships involve respect, consideration for others and trust that is earned. High school and college age young women all too often trust that a man will behave as a gentleman or "gentle man" during their interactions. Such blind trust can result in bad things happening to good people; their innocence is preyed upon. The techniques demonstrated in Common Sense Self-Defense are intended to help women protect themselves by applying simple yet effective self-defense tactics.

Improvised Weapons

Improvised Weapons

Improvised Weapons

Anything can be used as a weapon under extreme conditions.

Embracing this concept empowers you forever because it means you will never be completely helpless; a weapon will always be at your disposal. Start now thinking about how objects can be used as tools in your arsenal. Maximize the effectiveness of your improvised tool by being deliberate and focused when you execute. I selected a few that women in my training sessions identified as easy to execute regardless of each woman's height or weight.

- Your dinner napkin can be used to choke an attacker as Lana demonstrates on page 156, or flicked into his eye to disorient; or used to constrain.
- Cup of coffee to the eyes to distract.
- Ink pen or pencil to the eye, throat, and hand to cause injury.
- Mop or broom thrust into the attacker's solar plexus, groin, or ribs.
- A tightly rolled newspaper or magazine slapped across a perpetrator's eyes, throat, solar plexus, ribs or ears can stun.
- An umbrella to the groin, solar plexus, ribs, or throat allow you to attack and maintain a distance from an assailant.
- A portfolio thrust into someone's throat will stun. Slapping it across an attacker's wrist can cause him to release a knife.
- A wooden heel can be used like a hammer, while a stiletto heel can be used like a spike.

Improvised Weapons

Keys

Improvised Weapons

Please see photos page 158 for Lana's demonstration of the following:

- Keys serve a multitude of purposes as an improvised weapon. They can be used to stab an attacker in the hands to encourage him to release you.
- The abundance of keys is another reason a key is a good improvised weapon. Generally, keys are readily available.
- They may also be used to stab an attacker in the ears, face, eyes or under the chin. In a life threatening scenario a key can be used to incapacitate a perpetrator by stabbing his trachea or carotid artery.
- Kubotans are another handy tool. A kubotan is a self-defense key chain that is usually used to target bony, fleshy and nerve targets such as knuckles, forearms, bridge of the nose, shins, stomach, solar plexus, spine, temple, ribs, groin, neck, or eyes.
- Run away!

Improvised Weapons

Ink Pen

Improvised Weapons

Please see photos page 160 for Lana's demonstration of the following:

- An ink pen may be used to stab an attacker in the hands to encourage him to release you.
- Ink pens may also be used to stab an attacker in the face or in the eyes. They may also be used to attack the attacker's throat (trachea or underneath the chin).
- Run away!

Improvised Weapons

Portfolio

Improvised Weapons

Please see photos page 162 for Lana's demonstration of the following:

- A portfolio may be used to attack the attacker's throat.
- It may be used to slap the attacker in the face or down across the hands to prevent him from grabbing you or a loved one.
- It may be used to slap an attacker's wrist if he has a knife.
- Run away!

Improvised Weapons

The information on non lethal options is designed to help expose you to the variety of non lethal tools available on the market. The list does not serve as an endorsement by the author of their effectiveness. Also, the options listed are not comprehensive.

Chapter 11

Non Lethal Options

Pepper spray, tasers, stun guns, and impact flashlights only qualify as weapons if they are in your hand or readily accessible. Stuck in the bottom of your purse or console of your car don't count!

Non Lethal Options

Understanding Non Lethal Options

Pepper Spray

Pepper spray, like the milk in your refrigerator, has an expiration date. If it is part of your defense arsenal, it must be refreshed in accordance with the manufacture's instruction. If you have friends or other loved ones who carry pepper spray canisters, advise them today to check the expiration date. There are expired spray canisters resting at the bottom of purses across the country. A pepper spray canister with neutralized contents is only useful as an improvised weapon; it might be used to throw at a perpetrator to distract him.

Pepper spray is an inflammatory. It works by irritating mucous membranes in the eyes, nose, mouth and lungs, and causes crying, sneezing, coughing, hard breathing, pain in the eyes, temporary blindness. The duration of its effects depends on the strength of the spray. Without treatment the full effect lasts approximately thirty to forty-five minutes, with diminished effects lasting for hours.

Pepper spray typically comes in canisters, which are often small enough to be carried or concealed in a pocket or purse. Pepper spray can often been bought in highly concealable items such as rings or ink pens. Highly concealable pepper spray dispensers are usually effective only at very close range. The tool's name is derived from the active ingredient oleoresin capsicum (OC). OC derived from many of the hottest chili peppers in the world.

Non Lethal Options

Impact Flashlights

Impact flashlights are multi-use weapons. They can be used to temporary blind or disorient a person's night-adapted vision. Impact flashlights typically have hardened edges for use as a self-defense striking tool. They neutralize the threat via pain compliance. They are typically most effective at close ranges.

Non Lethal Options

Stun Guns

A stun gun is an electrical self-defense device that uses high voltage to stop an attacker. Touching a person with the prongs on the stun gun immobilizes quickly. The stun gun is designed to adversely impact the nervous system. It dumps its energy into the muscles at a high pulse frequency that makes the muscles work very rapidly, but not efficiently.

A stun gun is not the same as a taser. A stun gun is a direct-contact weapon. In contrast, a taser delivers electrical shock remotely by means of barbed contacts connected by wires. The user of a stun gun must be at closer range than the user of a taser for the tool to serve its intended purpose.

Tasers

A taser is a conducted energy weapon that utilizes compressed nitrogen to shoot two small probes up to 15 feet. These probes are connected to the weapon by high-voltage insulated wire. When the probes make contact with the target, the weapon transmits powerful electrical pulses along the wires and into the body of the target. It can totally incapacitate upon impact regardless of the body part it touches. Traditional firearms often require contact with a vital area to quickly neutralize a threat. In contrast to a hand gun, a taser's advantage is that it requires far less target practice to get the same result.

Non Lethal Options

Tasers are generally not designed to be used as direct contact weapons. One of their major advantages is providing protection from a distance. However, many are designed to be used in a direct contact mode.

Another advantage of a taser is that they have been shown to be reliable in taking down even the most aggressive person. A taser can even penetrate approximately two inches of clothing. Because of their extreme effectiveness, tasers are considered to be one of the best choices among non lethal defense weapons available to the public.

Non Lethal Options

Non Lethal Options

Sabre Self-Defense Pen

This handy pepper spray pen is easily concealable in a pocket or purse. It looks like a real ink pen; just remove the cap to fire. It contains red pepper; CS Military tear gas; and invisible ultraviolet light sensitive dye that aids police in identifying the attacker.

Targeted Stopping Area: Face

Stopping Technique: Pain Compliance

Effective Range: Up to 3 Feet

Non Lethal Options

Kimber Life Act Guardian Angel

The Guardian Angel emits two individual shots of a powerful OC mixture, capable of incapacitating an attacker for up to 45 minutes. It is easy to use and allows you to keep an attacker at a distance, as it can be discharged from 13 feet away. Powered by a pyrotechnic drive, the two independent charges travel at 90 mph and cover 13 feet in 1/10 of a second.

Targeted Stopping Area: Face

Stopping Technique: Pain Compliance

Effective Range: Up to 13 Feet

Non Lethal Options

SureFire Executive Defender Impact Flashlight

The Executive Defender provides 200 lumen of light which can be used to temporary blind an attacker an allow an escape or at minimum, provide time for you get off the line of attack. It also features a crenellated Strike Bezel and scalloped tail-cap provide two sets of hard-anodized aluminum "teeth" as an additional line of defense. It is small and compact and fits snuggly in a woman's hand. It is a good "take along tool" for work, jogging, shopping and traveling as it is often allowable in environments where traditional weapons are not permissible.

Targeted Stopping Area: Face , hands, legs, solar
                          plexus, temple and clavicle

Stopping Technique: Pain Compliance

Effective Range: Up to 3 Feet (for impact
                          feature), 5 -6 Feet (for light
                          feature)

Non Lethal Options

Blast Stun Knuckles

The Stun Knuckles are a non-traditional type of stun gun which allows you to maintain the use your hands. They function like a traditional stun gun by using voltage to initiate pain compliance. They feature a 950,000 volt charge. This device has a soft rubber skin and is sized to accommodate most hand sizes.

Targeted Stopping Area: Face , hands, legs, solar
                                 plexus, ribs, most body parts

Stopping Technique: Pain Compliance

Effective Range: Up to 3 Feet (arms length)

Non Lethal Options

Scorpion Stun Gun 400K

This 400,000 volt mini stun gun is one of the smallest, most powerful single battery 400k units on the market. The power is derived from a single 9 volt battery. The SP-400 includes a built in personal alarm and safety disconnect switch. The unit is 4-3/4" tall, 2-3/8" wide and 1-1/8" thick. It features a safety disconnect switch incorporated into the wrist strap. With the wrist strap around the hand; if the gun was taken away, it would be rendered useless until the pin is reinstalled. Rechargeable units use the pin hole as the recharging port.

Targeted Stopping Area: Face , hands, legs, solar plexus, ribs, most body parts

Stopping Technique: Pain Compliance

Effective Range: Up to 3 Feet (arms length)

Non Lethal Options

Taser International C2

TASER C2 lets you stop an attacker from up to 15 feet away. The TASER C2 relies on neuro muscular incapacitation not pain compliance (unless used in the stun gun capacity). Tasers jam sensory and motor functions, which inhibits muscular control.

Tasers allow you to target any area of an assailant's body, giving you a broader range of options to protect yourself in a stressful, dangerous situation.

Targeted Stopping Area: Anywhere on the body

Stopping Technique: Neuro Muscular
                            Incapacitation

Effective Range: Up to 15 Feet

Index

Confidence is Sexy!

29354644R00108

Made in the USA
Charleston, SC
10 May 2014